ROCKET!

How a Toy
Launched
the Space Age

Richard Maurer

Crown Publishers, Inc.
New York

To Robert and Ralph

....

Acknowledgments

Karen Shapiro of Holden, Massachusetts, got me thinking by asking me to organize a rocket program for "flight week" at Rice School. Dorothy Mosakowski of the Goddard Library at Clark University and the staff of the Gale Free Library in Holden helped in many ways. Frank H. Winter, curator of rocketry at the Smithsonian National Air and Space Museum, very kindly reviewed the manuscript and made several suggestions. Professors Nikolaos Gatsonis and Hamid Johari of Worcester Polytechnic Institute contributed technical advice. I am also indebted to the staff at Crown Publishers, notably editor-in-chief Simon Boughton, art director Isabel Warren-Lynch, and book designer Janet Pedersen. Faith Hamlin, my agent, was most helpful.

Photo and art credits are given on page 64, but I wish particularly to thank Andrew Davidhazy of Rochester Institute of Technology and Peter Harrington of Brown University—along with Matthew Van Fleet, who created the artwork, and William Enright, who designed and built the centrifugal-drive device illustrated on page 11, based on Goddard's youthful notes.

Susie, Sam, and Joe were once again indispensable.

This book is dedicated to my brothers, Robert and Ralph. Without NASA or the Soviets ever knowing, we ran a rival space program at the height of the Moon race.

Text copyright © 1995 by Richard Maurer

All rights reserved. No part of this book may be reproduced or transmitted in any form or by any means, electronic or mechanical, including photocopying, recording, or by any information storage and retrieval system, without permission in writing from the publisher.

Published by Crown Publishers, Inc., a Random House company, 201 East 50th Street, New York, New York 10022

CROWN is a trademark of Crown Publishers, Inc.

Manufactured in Hong Kong

Library of Congress Cataloging-in-Publication Data

Maurer, Richard, 1950–

Rocket! How a toy launched the space age / by Richard Maurer.

p. cm.

Includes index.

1. Rocketry—United States—History—Juvenile literature. 2. Goddard, Robert Hutchings, 1882–1945—Contributions in rocketry—Juvenile literature. 3. n–us. [1. Rocketry—History. 2. Goddard, Robert Hutchings, 1882–1945.] I. Title.

TL781.8.U5M3   1995

621.43'56'0973—dc20   94-19243

ISBN   0-517-59628-8 (trade)

0-517-59629-6 (lib. bdg.)

10   9   8   7   6   5   4   3   2   1

First Edition

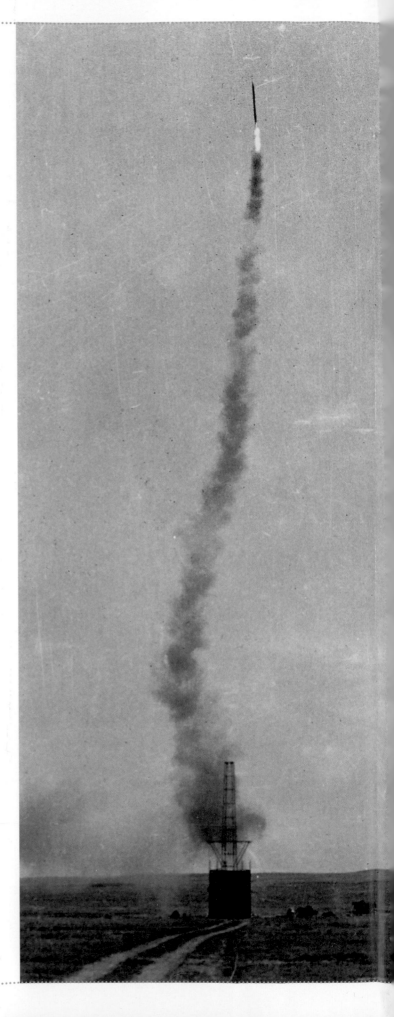

Goddard rocket, 1937.

Contents

An Unpromising Start

4

Incident in a Cherry Tree

7

Inventing Rocket Science

19

The Space Race Begins

32

To Earth Orbit . . . and Beyond

46

Resources

63

Index & Picture Credits

64

Space Shuttle, 1982.

An Unpromising Start

Don't mind these rockets, boys. They are mere toys to amuse children!

—General Andrew Jackson, at the Battle of New Orleans,
January 1815

The War of 1812 pitted the young United States against Great Britain in a sequel to the American Revolution, which had ended some thirty years earlier. With a powerful army and the world's largest navy, the British were confident of success this time. And they had a secret weapon: rockets.

Rockets were invented in China about a thousand years ago. First used as toys, they were soon adapted for warfare. War rockets were smoky, noisy, and, above all, scary. Most were a foot or two long (30–60 cm), not counting the launching stick. When they went off, people who had never seen one were terrified: "It was like a thunderbolt from the heavens; it seemed as if a dragon flew through the air," wrote an astonished witness in the 1200s.

But rockets were not very accurate. They could start serious fires and cause explosions when they hit where they were supposed to hit, but

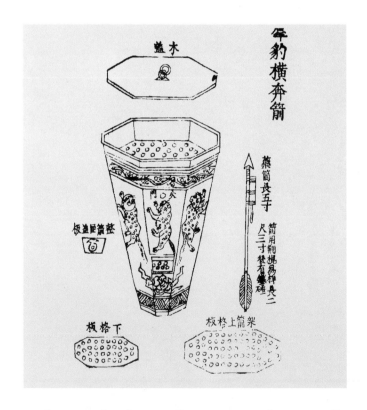

▲ One use of rockets in China was to make arrows fly farther than they would if shot by bow. These "fire arrows" were not too precise. Many had to be fired at once—from the leopard-decorated launcher—to have any effect. This illustration is from 1628.

▲ War rockets (seen in the distance) were fired at the Battle of Waterloo in 1815, at which Napoleon's French Army was defeated by the British and their allies. The British commander was reluctant to use them, having said at a previous battle, "I do not want to set fire to any town, and I do not know any other use of rockets."

few did. A close cousin of the rocket—the gun—was far more effective. Introduced several centuries after rockets, guns were considered a great improvement, since they could be used repeatedly and were more accurate.

Even so, inventors kept trying to improve rockets. By the War of 1812, a British army officer named William Congreve had developed versions weighing more than 30 pounds (14 kg), capable of traveling about two miles (3 km). When these missiles struck their targets, they burst into flames or exploded, depending on the type. Hundreds of Congreve rockets were fired against Fort McHenry, Maryland, on the night of September 13–14, 1814. An American eyewitness, Francis Scott Key, described "the rockets' red glare" in a poem he wrote about the attack. Put to music, Key's poem became the American national anthem. Its words tell the disappointing story of Great Britain's secret weapon: the flag flew and the fort held throughout the bombardment; rockets put on quite a show, but achieved little.

▲ *Rockets continued to play a minor role in warfare throughout the 1800s. Here, British troops practice firing a rocket launcher in the 1840s.*

Disappointed by their entire campaign, the British agreed to make peace in December 1814. News traveled slowly in those days, and one more major battle would be fought in ignorance of the war's end. During late December 1814 and early January 1815, the British tried again and again to capture the port city of New Orleans, Louisiana. General Andrew Jackson's backwoods militia withstood all the British could throw at them—including rockets.

"They hoped that its very noise would strike terror into us," an American officer wrote after a rocket attack. "But we soon grew accustomed to it."

Obviously, rockets were not well suited for winning wars—much less, it seemed, for anything else.

Incident in a Cherry Tree

The War of 1812 was fought with muzzle-loading muskets, wooden sailing ships, smooth-bore cannons, and rockets. By the end of the century, technology had transformed warfare. Machine guns, steel-plated steamships, rifled artillery, and high-explosive shells were the standard weapons. Rockets had all but been abandoned.

The deadly new armaments were produced in factories run by the latest power-producing machines: steam engines. Industries powered by steam were transforming almost every other aspect of society. Trains, gaslights, telegraph equipment, automated looms, new farming tools, mass-produced books and newspapers, and countless other inventions created in factories were changing the way people lived. After centuries when practically nothing changed, people began to see change everywhere. Suddenly, they began to think about the future. They knew it was going to be different—very different.

▲ *In 1898, the latest word in warfare was the U.S. Asiatic Fleet, which sank the Spanish squadron in Manila Bay during the opening days of the Spanish-American War. It was the first big battle between ships with steel hulls, steam power, and long-range artillery.*

▲ *Jules Verne's bullet ship blasts off in* From the Earth to the Moon.

▲ *The future of space travel, as envisioned in Verne's novel.*

Space Stories

One way that people could imagine the future was by reading a new type of entertainment: science fiction. Here were stories about time travel, death rays, flying machines, submarines, robots, monsters produced in the lab, and other forecasts of fantastic things to come.

The most popular science fiction stories were about space travel. Much of Earth had been explored by the late 1800s, and space offered the next frontier, a frontier that had already been glimpsed through powerful new telescopes.

Certainly no one knew how to get into space, but that didn't stop authors from writing about it. Their imaginations ran wild. They used flying bicycles, fast-growing beanstalks, merry-go-rounds, catapults, balloons, bombs, giant springs, flocks of birds, and, in one story, a surprised leap from an ice-cold bath.

Authors who were serious about sounding scientific usually resorted to magnetism, electricity, or antigravity substances. They almost never bothered to explain how these techniques worked, since they had no idea; but it didn't seem to matter, as long as the methods *sounded* as though they would work.

However, some authors were careful to pick methods that might really work. In *From the Earth to the Moon*, published in 1865, the French author Jules Verne propelled his characters into space in a bullet ship fired from a giant gun. Verne was immensely popular, particularly among scientists, who were impressed with his imaginative use of scientific facts and principles. *From the Earth to the Moon* was no exception. However, some experts did point out that the crew of the bullet ship would not have been able to survive the violent acceleration of launch.

In 1897, the English writer H. G. Wells also called in the artillery for his story *The War of the Worlds*, in which Martians invade England aboard giant artillery shells fired from the Red Planet. The tale was so lifelike and exciting that some newspapers published daily installments. A few even changed the setting to match the places where the newspapers were read. No one claimed the story was true, but Wells's vivid writing made space travel come to life.

Robert Goddard Climbs a Tree

In Worcester, Massachusetts, a sixteen-year-old boy named Robert Goddard anxiously awaited each new installment of *Fighters from Mars, or The War of the Worlds, in and near Boston*, as the *Boston Post* retitled Wells's book. The series appeared in January 1898, and it made a deep impression on the youth.

Almost two years later, on October 19, 1899, the memory of the story returned to Goddard as he climbed a cherry tree in his backyard. Armed

▲ *Robert Goddard and his mother in an apple tree, around 1900.*

▲ *The cherry tree behind Goddard's home, about the time he got the idea for a spaceship while pruning its branches. Note the homemade ladder with the saw on the top rungs.*

Obeying Newton's Laws

The space vehicle that Goddard had imagined while in the cherry tree was supposed to lift itself by whirling a fixed weight around and around a horizontal shaft. Goddard reasoned that if the weight moved more rapidly at the top of its arc, the vehicle would rise because of the greater force on that side. He built several models to test the idea, but the devices didn't go anywhere.

Goddard's mistake was failing to realize that one force balances another. When you swing a stone on a string, the tug you feel in your arms as the stone revolves around and around is the outward reaction of the weight to your inward pull on it. It feels as if the stone is trying to pull you away. But the force the stone exerts in an outward direction exactly balances the force you exert inwardly. The faster you swing the stone, the harder you have to pull.

This counterbalancing of forces was first described in the late 1600s by the English scientist Isaac Newton. Newton wanted to explain all motion in the universe in terms of a few simple principles, or laws. His first law of motion describes the tendency of objects at rest to stay at rest, and of objects in motion to stay in motion. His second law deals with the close connection between force (a push or a pull), mass (the amount of matter, or "stuff," in something), and acceleration (the rate at which something changes speed).

Newton's third law describes the forces between objects, and it states: "To every action there is always opposed an equal reaction." By

with a saw and a hatchet, he was intending to prune a few branches. Instead, he ended up gazing into the distance and thinking about *The War of the Worlds*.

Sitting in the tree, just a few feet off the ground, he became convinced that travel between the planets was actually possible. In his imagination, he began to construct the machine he thought could do it. Many years later, he recalled that on descending the ladder, "I was a different boy."

Almost every year for the rest of his life he noted the anniversary of that sunny October afternoon when he neglected his chores, just for a moment, and saw the future.

◄ *Isaac Newton (1647–1727), honored on a recent British banknote.*

"action" and "reaction," Newton meant a force and a balancing force. Newton's third law explains why Goddard's whirling contraption would not fly. The forces were balanced in all directions. Therefore, everything stayed exactly where it was.

Goddard later admitted that following these disappointing experiments, "I began to think that there might be something after all to Newton's laws."

▼ *Goddard's whirling-weight contraption. The machine can't lift itself up because it's pushing itself down at the same time. This drawing is based on Goddard's description of his working—or rather, unworking—model.*

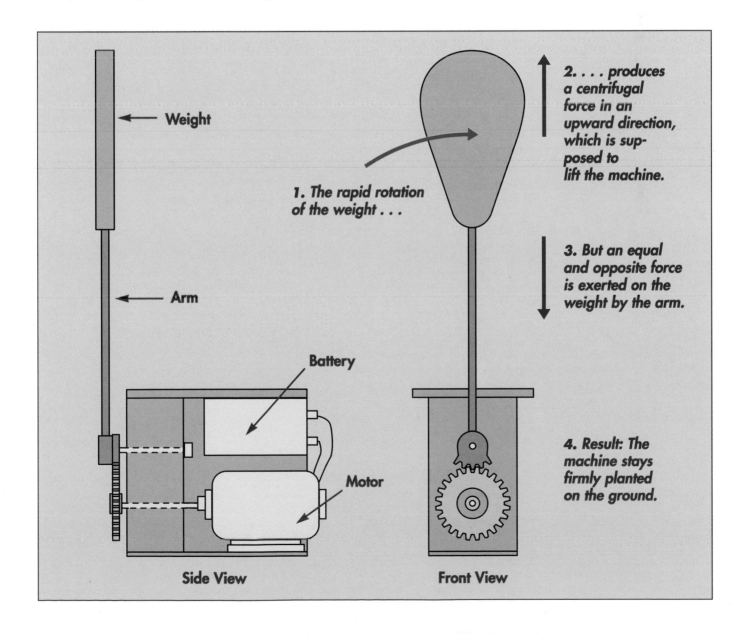

Weight

Arm

Battery

Motor

Side View

1. The rapid rotation of the weight . . .

2. . . . produces a centrifugal force in an upward direction, which is supposed to lift the machine.

3. But an equal and opposite force is exerted on the weight by the arm.

4. Result: The machine stays firmly planted on the ground.

Front View

"What time will it be the end of the world?"

On the night before Halloween, 1938, millions of radio listeners tuned in to a performance of *The War of the Worlds*. Like the version Goddard read in the newspapers forty years earlier, the story was presented as if it were actually happening. The only trouble was, radio actor-director Orson Welles succeeded too well.

In spite of several announcements that the program was "only a play," many people became alarmed at the bulletins of mysterious sightings on Mars, strange machines arriving on Earth, and mass destruction by aliens. The program even broadcast an emergency statement from a man who sounded like the president of the United States. More than a million people took the play literally and believed that Martians were landing.

"Someone turned on the radio," remembered a man who was attending a party. "It was just when the Martians were spraying the people . . . with the heat ray. At first we couldn't believe it was happening, but it was so real we stayed glued to the radio getting more and more scared every minute." The man sped away by car to warn his family and friends. Thousands of others also took to the roads, not sure where to go since according to the broadcast Martians were landing everywhere. Telephone lines were jammed. One caller got through to a newspaper and pleaded, "What time will it be the end of the world?"

Mass panics are hard to explain. But in the early part of the twentieth century, people had seen so much technological change (including the introduction of radio), and had been exposed to so much bad news of wars and revolutions, that a riveting story presented in a clever way was enough to convince many of them that invaders from space had really arrived.

◀ *Since its first publication in 1897,* The War of the Worlds *has been enduringly popular. Here, the story's Martian war machines march across the cover of a 1927 science fiction magazine.*

What Is Force?

Getting off the ground and into space clearly requires a great deal of force. In *From the Earth to the Moon* and *The War of the Worlds*, this force is applied all at once in a tremendous explosion at the bottom of a gun barrel. You can think of this force as a huge push—enough to overcome the force, or pull, of gravity.

Scientists define force in terms of the amount of motion a given push or pull will produce. Nothing *has* to move for force to be involved. When you step off a diving board, the force of gravity pulls you toward Earth. When you lie in bed, the force of gravity is still pulling, even though you aren't falling. When you push against a house, the house doesn't go anywhere, although if you push hard enough—with a bulldozer—it will.

How do you measure force? When you stand on a bathroom scale, you are measuring the force that gravity exerts on you, a force we call "weight." You can place the same scale against a wall, lean on it, and measure the force you exert against the building. Push harder, and the scale records a greater force.

Bathroom scales measure force in units of pounds or kilograms. We will use these same units in this book, since they immediately tell whether a given force will move a given mass off Earth's surface. For example, a force of more than 220 pounds (100 kg) will lift a 220-pound (100-kg) football player off the ground. Goddard knew that if his spaceship weighed, say, one ton (2,000 pounds—or 900 kg), then he must exert a force greater than one ton, for a considerable period of time, in order to get his vehicle off the ground and into space. (Scientists usually measure force in "newtons," a metric unit named after Isaac Newton. One newton is equal to 0.22 pound—or 0.1 kg—on a bathroom scale and corresponds to the force that will accelerate one kilogram of mass one meter per second every second. It takes an average force of about one newton to give a baseball a fairly gentle toss.)

Search for a Solution

In his search for a solution to the problem of space flight, Goddard was influenced by the stunning success of technology in his day. To a society that had harnessed science for countless new uses, almost anything seemed possible. Surely a simple and ingenious method of space travel would turn up! After all, steam-powered locomotives had made trips between American cities almost miraculously easy. And beginning in the 1870s, the brilliant inventor Thomas Edison had turned out one remarkable gadget after another, including the phonograph and the electric light, each based on simple scientific principles. Wouldn't space travel prove just as easy once the "trick" was found?

Goddard had several hunches what the trick might be. Taking to heart Newton's action-reaction principle, he reasoned that if one of the poles of a magnet could be somehow switched off or shielded, the resulting unbalanced force would create a reaction that would propel the magnet forever. After serious thought, Goddard concluded that there was "no known method of

Big Guns

Jules Verne carefully calculated the shell size, barrel length, muzzle velocity, and other specifications for the space gun he used in *From the Earth to the Moon*.

In reality, his bullet ship would have emerged from the cannon in a violent explosion of hot gases—and plopped, smoldering and wrecked, nearby. Verne had failed to account for the air in the barrel, which would have to move out of the way of the rapidly accelerating shell. The air would have been compressed and heated. And the shell, trapped between the exploding propellant below and the dense air above, would in all likelihood have been flattened and partially melted. Anyone aboard would have been flattened, too.

But there are ways to make Verne's cannon work. Recently, engineers at Lawrence Livermore National Laboratory in California have tested a big gun, 155 feet (47 m) long, that solves the air-in-the-barrel problem—by removing the air. The air is pumped out, and the opening of the barrel is capped with a thin piece of plastic. The shell glides easily through the vacuum and punctures the plastic on its way out.

▲ The "big gun" at Lawrence Livermore National Laboratory in California blasts a shell into its usual target: a hillside. The "shell" in this 1993 test was an experimental aircraft engine, fired to determine if it would work at enormously high speed.

▲ *The space gun in* From the Earth to the Moon.

Shells from the big gun are propelled by compressed gas—just like BBs in an air rifle. The shells, which are about the size of a small fireplace log, have reached speeds that could easily take them briefly into space, though so far the gun has been confined to horizontal tests. Someday a bigger version of the big gun may actually launch satellites that are sturdy enough to stand the high acceleration of this mode of travel—though humans will never be able to go along without getting flattened.

accomplishing this at present." Indeed, it is impossible.

He experimented with gyroscopes. Like spinning tops, gyroscopes seem to exert a force that resists the pull of gravity. In his search for a means of harnessing this force for propulsion, Goddard was again unsuccessful. Again, it can't be done, because the forces of a gyroscope must always be in balance. (Years later, Goddard would find gyroscopes useful for *guiding* space vehicles.)

Many times he despaired of ever succeeding. He recorded his frustrations in a notebook, writing one day, "There may be some trick of applying things that are known, or there may be something that is not known . . . but at present the thing is impossible."

Still, he kept searching. He knew that Verne's cannon-fired space vehicle would have killed the crew with its tremendous acceleration and that, in addition, the ship would have melted from air friction as it shot through the atmosphere at fantastic speed. But what if the *gun* instead of the bullet was the space vehicle? Goddard had often gone target shooting with his father, and he knew what happens when a gun is fired: it recoils. The recoil is the equal and opposite reaction to the force of the bullet leaving the firing chamber. Goddard reasoned that if bullets were fired repeatedly, then the reaction force might be enough to propel the gun aloft. Furthermore, the acceleration would not be so great as to harm the crew or ship. Could this be the trick?

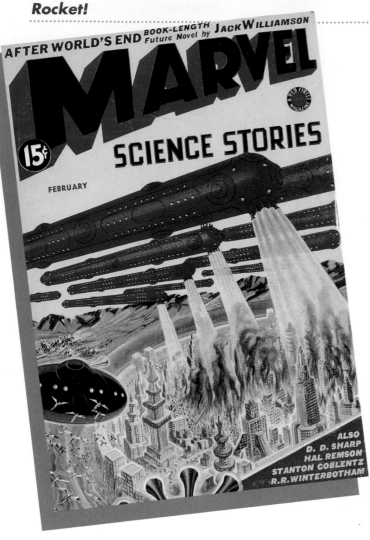

▲ *Powered by "cosmical repulsion," red interstellar cruisers destroy the city of Achnor on the planet Meldoon in a 1939 novel by Jack Williamson. The black saucer at the lower left is kept aloft by "space-contraction drive," an older technology, according to the story. Goddard tried unsuccessfully to find equally convenient (and, as it happened, equally impossible) power sources for a space vehicle.*

The Trick

A rifle fired straight down will produce enough recoil to jerk itself upward slightly—about one inch (2.5 cm) for a .22-caliber rifle. This is amazing if you think about it. A lightweight bullet can make a heavy gun defy gravity, just for a moment. The reason is the incredible speed of the bullet. According to Newton's third law, a lightweight object moving rapidly in one direc-

tion can make a heavy object move somewhat more slowly in the other.

In his imagination, Goddard pictured a ship of guns firing continuously all the way into space. Unlike Verne's cannon, this was something that might really work. But the more he thought about it, the less workable it seemed. Each shot of the gun would add a little more speed, but the number of shots would have to be enormous. The ship would have to consist almost entirely of ammunition. Everything else about it—including the gun barrel—would have to be reduced in weight to make room for bullets. However, it isn't safe to make gun barrels too light, since they have to be sturdy and heavy to keep from bursting when fired.

So Goddard looked elsewhere for an unknown trick—a new idea—that would make it all easy. By 1905, he had graduated from high school and was enrolled at Worcester Polytechnic Institute, a local technical college. Well aware that mathematics and physics held the key to his dream, Goddard worked hard at these subjects, applying his new knowledge to the problem of space flight.

He learned about the latest scientific discoveries: radio waves, electric fields, radioactivity, and solar energy. In his spare time, he tried each of these principles in his search for the trick. Nothing seemed to work. "Decided that space navigation is a physical impossibility," he wrote after two years at college. But he was soon back on the trail. Almost anyone else would have given up, if not after a year, then after two, three, or four. But Goddard kept scribbling new ideas

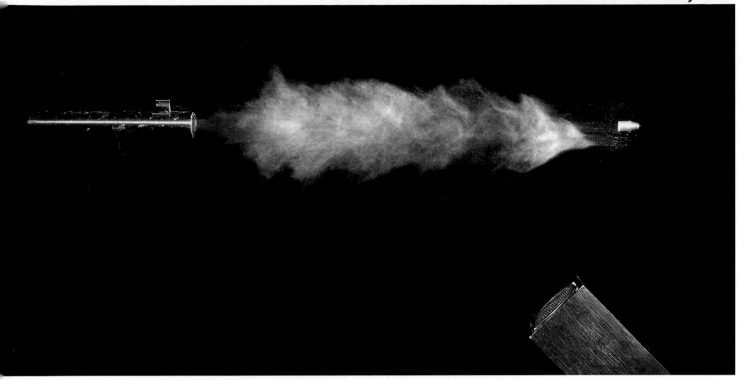

▲ *A bullet leaves a .22-caliber rifle at high speed. Newton's third law gives the rifle a jolt in the opposite direction.*

◀ *A state-of-the-art rocket in 1909, the year Goddard determined that rockets were the only hope for getting into space.*

in his notebook long, long after that sunny afternoon in the cherry tree.

Slowly, it began to dawn on him: Suppose something like a gun is used, but with a stubby, sawed-off barrel. Instead of bullets, a slow-burning, energetic explosive would shoot high-speed gases out the barrel, driving the vehicle by reaction, just as a speeding bullet does. The gases would produce the same recoil effect as bullets, and this new type of engine would be much lighter than a gun, and far more powerful.

Goddard realized that it was not new at all.

It was a rocket.

Inventing Rocket Science

On March 13, 1913, a large crowd in Jersey City, New Jersey, watched in amazement as a stuntman named Rodman Law climbed atop a giant fireworks rocket 44 feet (14 m) high, settled into a seat, checked his parachute, and announced confidently, "You may light the fuse when ready, Sam!"

Law was famous for this sort of thing. A few months earlier, he had taken a balloon aloft and exploded it with dynamite while escaping by parachute. This time, he intended to streak half a mile (0.8 km) skyward and bail out.

But instead of soaring to thousands of feet, the vehicle blew into thousands of pieces. Miraculously, Law survived, but his attempt did nothing to help the reputation of rockets.

How Rockets Work

Meanwhile, Goddard was teaching physics at Princeton University. He would soon join the faculty at Clark University in Worcester, where he would be a professor for most of the rest of his life. Lecturing on Newton's laws by day, he put those same laws to work at night by designing rockets. As Rodman Law had so convincingly

Opposite: Holding a nose cone to place over his head, daredevil Rodman Law prepares to ride a giant skyrocket in 1913. **Above:** *Law's rocket explodes. He survived to perform other stunts—though none with rockets.*

demonstrated, rockets needed many improvements before they could be used for space flight.

The idea of a rocket is very simple. Like a gun, it shoots matter in one direction and recoils in the opposite direction. The "matter" is not bullets but exhaust gases, produced by whatever fuel the rocket burns. Gases are composed of molecules, which can be thought of as tiny bullets. The more of these "bullets" there are, and the faster they go, the greater will be the recoil of the rocket. The most powerful rocket is the one with the most energetic fuel that shoots the most gas molecules at the highest speed.

Actually, fuel is only part of what makes a rocket go. For anything to burn, an "oxidizer" is normally needed along with the fuel. An oxidizer is oxygen or a chemical with oxygen that combines with the fuel to make it burn. Together, the fuel and oxidizer are called the "propellant." In a gunpowder rocket, like Rodman Law's, the fuel is mainly a form of carbon called charcoal. (Sugar also works in such rockets, since it, too, is mostly carbon.) When you burn charcoal in an outdoor grill, the oxidizer is simply the oxygen in the air.

In gunpowder, the oxidizer is a chemical called potassium nitrate, which makes the charcoal burn much more quickly than it does in air. Law's problem may have been that he used too much oxidizer, which made the propellant burn so quickly that it exploded.

Because rockets carry their own oxidizer, they can operate where there is no air: in space. This feature helped convince Goddard that rockets were perfect for his purpose.

How Rockets *Don't* Work

But others were not so convinced. Whenever Goddard suggested that a rocket might be used to get into space, he was often told that rockets couldn't possibly work in space because the exhaust gases would have nothing to push against. These critics misunderstood Newton's third law.

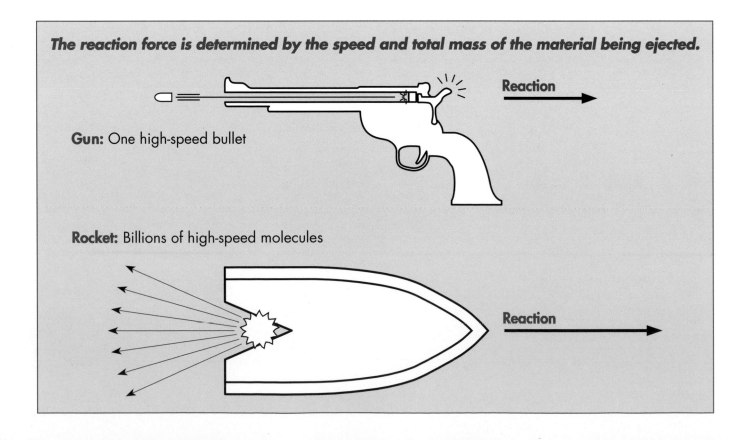

The reaction force is determined by the speed and total mass of the material being ejected.

Gun: One high-speed bullet

Reaction

Rocket: Billions of high-speed molecules

Reaction

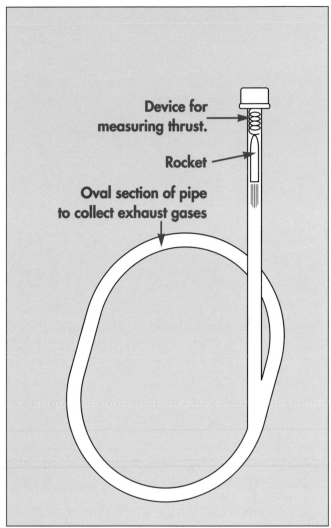

Device for measuring thrust.

Rocket

Oval section of pipe to collect exhaust gases

▲ *Goddard with the apparatus he used to prove that rockets can produce thrust in a vacuum. After attaching a rocket to a device that measured thrust, he removed the air. When the rocket was set off, the oval section trapped the exhaust gases, preventing them from rebounding up the pipe and affecting the measurement.*

First, let's consider Newton's third law when it applies to a gun:

STEP 1. AN EXPLOSION PUSHES A BULLET FROM A GUN AT HIGH SPEED.

STEP 2. THE BULLET PUSHES THE GUN IN REACTION, MAKING IT RECOIL.

(These steps happen simultaneously, but it's useful to think of them separately.) So far, so good.

Now let's consider what Goddard's critics *thought* was happening with a rocket:

STEP A. BURNING PROPELLANT PUSHES EXHAUST FROM A ROCKET AT HIGH SPEED.

STEP B. THE EXHAUST PUSHES AGAINST THE AIR BENEATH THE ROCKET, MAKING THE ROCKET GO IN THE OPPOSITE DIRECTION.

Step B is wrong. The exhaust gases don't need

Balloon Rockets

You can build your own force meter and use it to measure the thrust produced as air escapes from a balloon. You can also use the meter to weigh small objects.

Materials

- Plastic ruler with holes in the middle
- Two paper clips (1 regular size, 1 large size)
- Rubber band (a very stretchy one)
- Two pieces of drinking straw: about 3 in. (7.5 cm) long and 1¼ in. (3 cm) long
- Tape
- Post-it note (removable stick-on tag)
- Sandwich bag
- U.S. pennies (dated 1983 or later)
- Balloons
- Safety pin

1. Building the meter

- Unfold the regular-size paper clip to make an S shape. Attach the top hook to the top hole of the ruler.
- Cut the rubber band and tie one end to the bottom hook of the paper clip.
- Thread the rubber band through the long straw. Push the straw snugly onto the paper clip. Tape the straw to the center groove of the ruler.
- Bend apart the large paper clip to make a "Γ" shape. Tie the loose end of the rubber band to the top corner of the Γ. (The rubber band should be slightly stretched so that it pulls the Γ snugly against the straw. You may have to

shorten the straw if the rubber band is too short.)

- Thread the short piece of straw halfway up the Γ and tape it in place. Then bend the bottom of the Γ to make a hook.
- Attach a stick-on tag to the back of the ruler so that the top bar of the Γ (the "pointer") rests near the top of the tag.

2. Calibrating the meter

- Attach the sandwich bag to the bottom hook of the Γ.
- Mark the position of the pointer with "0" on the stick-on tag (the "scale").
- Drop two pennies in the bag. Mark the new position on the scale with "5." Drop in two more pennies; mark "10." Continue dropping in two pennies at a time, until there are 20 pennies total and you have reached the "50" mark. Because all U.S. pennies since 1983 weigh 2.5 gm each, you have created a weight scale in grams. (Multiply grams by 0.035 to get ounces. It takes 28.35 gm to equal 1 oz.)

3. Measuring thrust

- Attach the safety pin to the neck of a balloon and hook it to the meter.
- Move the scale so that the pointer reads "0." Now you can measure the balloon's thrust alone, having accounted for its weight.
- Detach the balloon, blow it up, hook it to the meter, and let go! Don't forget to watch the pointer.

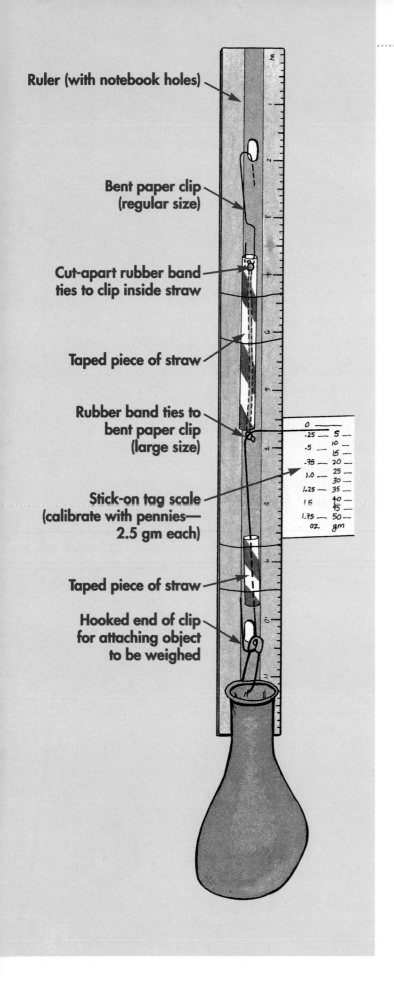

Ruler (with notebook holes)

Bent paper clip
(regular size)

Cut-apart rubber band
ties to clip inside straw

Taped piece of straw

Rubber band ties to
bent paper clip
(large size)

Stick-on tag scale
(calibrate with pennies—
2.5 gm each)

Taped piece of straw

Hooked end of clip
for attaching object
to be weighed

to push against the air, the ground, or anything else. The simple fact that gases are forced in one direction causes the rocket to go in the other direction in reaction. The gases are already pushing the rocket, in the same way that a bullet pushes a gun. This is true in air, in space, in water, or anywhere. Goddard must have heard about Step B so often that he decided to test a rocket in an airless chamber just to make sure it would work. He put together a long airtight pipe in his lab at Clark. He rigged one end with a spring on the inside to measure the force, or "thrust," produced by a small rocket after a vacuum pump had removed the air. If Step B were correct, a rocket in a vacuum would produce exhaust gases but no thrust. Instead, Goddard found that the rocket produced plenty of thrust. In fact, it produced *more* thrust than it did in air. (The reason is that air gets in the way of the exhaust and slows it down.) Goddard had proved that the principle that makes a rocket work is Newton's third law, pure and simple. Nothing else is required. He had also shown that if only a rocket could get above the atmosphere, into space, it would work best of all.

A Bigger Bang

As soon as he realized that rockets offered the best chance for getting into space, Goddard began to search for propellants that would produce more thrust for less weight than gunpowder. Thrust is determined by the amount of exhaust and its speed. Since the amount of exhaust simply depends on the amount of propellant, the best way to compare different propellants is to look at the *speed* of their exhaust.

When gunpowder or some other propellant is burned, its atoms rearrange themselves to form new molecules. In the process, they create a great deal of heat energy. Heat makes things expand, and the newly created molecules shoot away in all directions. By containing the expanding gases and allowing them to move in only one direction, a stream of very high speed exhaust is produced. The speed is called the "exhaust velocity," and it depends in part on the temperature of the burning chemicals. The higher the temperature, the greater the expansion from the released heat energy, and the greater the exhaust velocity.

Gunpowder burns at about 2,500° Fahrenheit (1,400° C), and it produces an exhaust velocity of up to 2,000 feet per second (600 m/s).

When Goddard tested the most efficient gunpowder rockets available, he found they produced about half the exhaust velocity that gunpowder *should* produce. The problem was that much of the energy of the expanding gases was wasted as the exhaust spewed out the back of the rocket in a wide plume. Goddard knew that by narrowing the plume and allowing the gases to expand at a smooth, steady rate, he could achieve closer to the ideal exhaust velocity. A device already existed to do this: the nozzle used

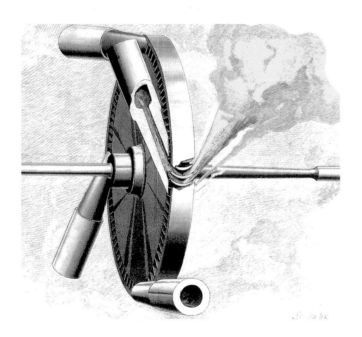

Above: A steam turbine designed in the 1890s by Swedish engineer Carl de Laval. The cutaway view of the nozzle shows how steam (shown in blue) is funneled through a narrow opening and then allowed to expand before striking the curved blades of the turbine wheel. The narrowing and then widening of the nozzle causes the jet of steam to reach a very high speed. Right: Goddard holding a de Laval nozzle that he converted into a rocket, proving that the nozzle would greatly improve exhaust speeds.

to direct high-pressure steam against turbine blades in power-generating equipment.

By using a steam nozzle and a different type of propellant—nitrocellulose, which is similar to nitroglycerin and burns at a much higher temperature than gunpowder—Goddard was able to get exhaust velocities of about 7,000 feet per second (2,100 m/s)—almost 4,800 miles per hour (7,700 km/h) and more than three times the performance of gunpowder.

This impressive result should not be confused with the speed of the rocket. A rifle shoots bullets at very high speed, but the recoil of the rifle is far less. The same is true of a rocket, especially

▲ *Today's rocket nozzles, such as those on the Space Shuttle, are almost always bell-shaped.*

when it is just starting out. However, while a rifle only fires a few rounds, a rocket fires its "ammunition" continuously, and it will keep picking up speed as long as gases are shooting out the back.

Escape Artist

Goddard had calculated that in order to escape the pull of Earth's gravity and reach the Moon or Mars, a rocket would have to achieve an "escape velocity" of about 25,000 miles per hour (40,000 km/h). Could such fantastic speeds be possible?

In *From the Earth to the Moon*, the characters explode hundreds of tons of propellant all at once at the bottom of a giant gun barrel and reach escape velocity in an instant. A spaceship needs to accelerate quickly, but not *that* quickly. For a spaceship to escape Earth's gravity without burning up from air friction or killing its crew from acceleration, it must accelerate gradually. But if the propellant is burned gradually, then much of it is used just to lift more propellant. When a car is driven with a full tank of gasoline, a portion of the fuel it burns is devoted to carrying gasoline that will be used later in the trip; a car actually gets the best fuel economy when its tank is almost empty. The situation is far more serious in a rocket, which does not simply roll around on Earth's surface like a car. A rocket must propel itself off the ground and fight gravity until it escapes—all on a single tank of gas. (There are no filling stations on the way up.) During the early portion of a rocket flight, *most* of the propellant is devoted to lifting propellant that will be used later in the flight. It seems

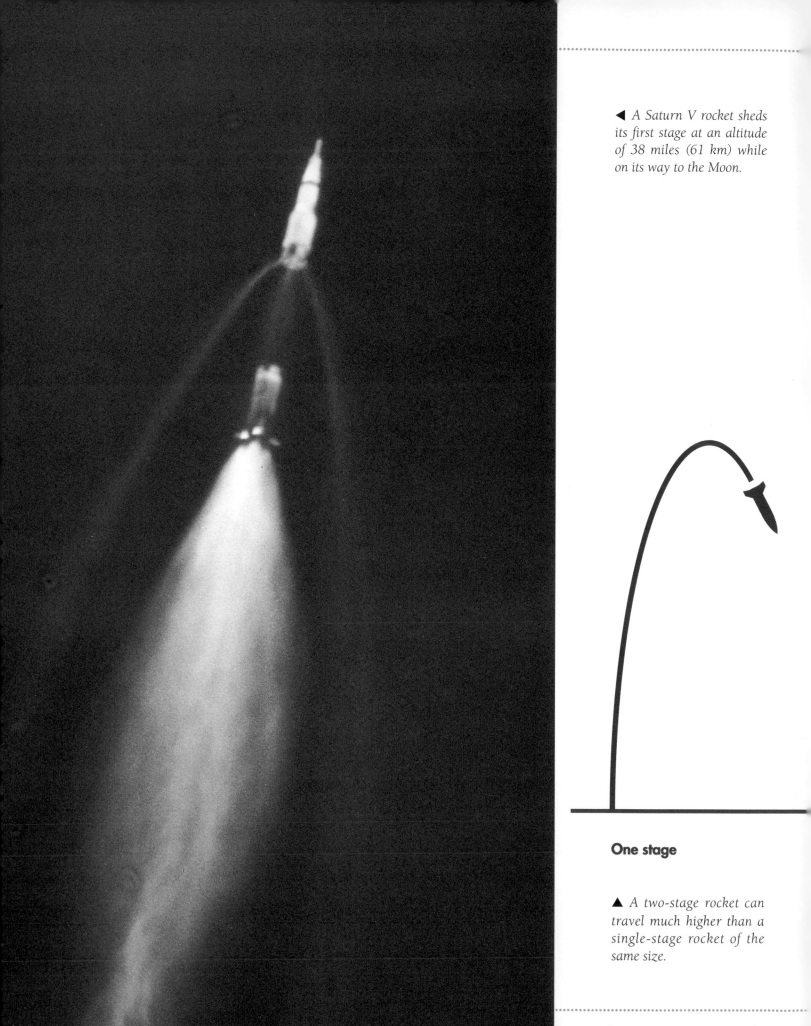

◀ A Saturn V rocket sheds its first stage at an altitude of 38 miles (61 km) while on its way to the Moon.

One stage

▲ A two-stage rocket can travel much higher than a single-stage rocket of the same size.

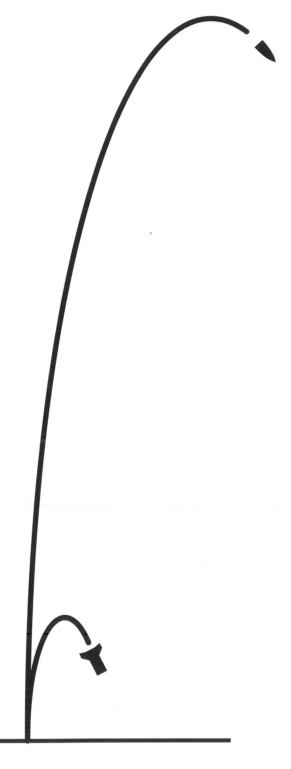

Two stages

a waste, but there is no way around it. When Goddard began calculating the amount of propellant required to reach escape velocity, he found that a gunpowder rocket like Rodman Law's would have to weigh more than the entire Earth just to struggle into space! No wonder most scientists thought space flight was a crazy dream.

However, Goddard's calculations also showed that the amount of propellant needed drops sharply as the rocket's exhaust velocity increases. A rocket powered by nitrocellulose can reach about 40 percent of escape velocity *if* 90 percent of its weight is propellant. (For comparison, less than 3 percent of the weight of a fully fueled car is gasoline.) Obviously, this is not yet fast enough, but Goddard had a trick to make a rocket go even faster. Suppose that several rockets are stacked together. The biggest rocket, at the bottom, starts out pushing the entire stack. When it runs out of propellant, it drops away. Then the next rocket takes over, adding even more speed. Then the third rocket takes over, and so on. By shedding weight as it is no longer needed, a rocket can reach almost any speed, as long as it starts out big enough.

According to Goddard's figures, a combination of "stages" like this would require about 600 pounds (270 kg) of nitrocellulose to push an object weighing one pound (0.45 kg) to escape velocity. A one-ton (900-kg) spaceship, sufficient to carry one person, would therefore need about 600 tons (540,000 kg) of propellant. It would take a train to deliver all that propellant, and an enormous rocket to

Fins

An arrow will start to tumble in flight unless it is equipped with fins. Fins produce a seesaw effect that catches air when the projectile is out of alignment and pivots it back to centered flight. A guide stick on a skyrocket (such as Rodman Law's, see page 18) serves the same purpose—although fins perform the job much more efficiently.

Fins also work well on rockets, not just to keep them flying straight but also to steer them on complicated flight paths. The steering is accomplished by pivoting the fins, much like operating the rudder of a boat.

Rockets without fins stabilize and steer themselves by pivoting the rocket's nozzle to change the direction of thrust, or by using small steering rockets called vernier rockets. This technique is a little like balancing a broom on its handle: small corrections produce big effects.

Some rockets, such as the Saturn V use fins *and* movable nozzles. The advantage is that if the nozzles malfunction, the fins can keep the rocket from tumbling. In the case of the Saturn V, which launched astronauts to the Moon, the presence of fins allowed the crew time to fire an escape rocket in case of steering trouble. Fortunately, such trouble never came.

▲ *A Saturn V with one of its fins visible.*

▲ *Like an arrow shot from a bow, this Astrobee rocket takes off in a burst of speed, using fins to keep it stable.*

◄ *Moments after liftoff in 1959, this Juno II rocket lost the ability to use its nozzle for steering. Even fins would not have helped, since the rocket was moving too slowly at this point for fins to have an effect.*

hold it, but it was not just a crazy dream. It was possible.

An Unexpected Letter

Perhaps it was possible, but space travel was also highly improbable in an age when few scientists would take it seriously. What was Goddard to do? His thoughts and calculations could range throughout the universe, but the expense of experimenting kept his actual tests confined to the laboratory. So far, his rockets were not even as impressive as those General Jackson had scorned at the Battle of New Orleans.

World War I changed this—briefly. The war started among the countries of Europe in 1914. Because of the improved technology of firearms, casualties mounted at a horrendous rate. When the United States entered the conflict in 1917, American military leaders were willing to pay for any new weapon that might give them an advantage over the enemy—even an improved version of an old, unreliable weapon. "We thought it was going to be some kind of toy," admitted one very surprised but enthusiastic officer after Goddard put on a demonstration of rockets he had developed for the U.S. Army. Even General Jackson would have been impressed if he could have seen the Worcester professor's tube-launched missile that a single soldier could carry, aim, and fire, with a good chance of hitting the target. But it would never see action, since the war ended in November 1918, just a few weeks after Goddard's field tests. With it ended the military's renewed interest in rockets.

▲ *Goddard loads his rocket launcher in a field test for the U.S. Army in 1918. Note the similarity to the British launcher on page 6.*

▲ *Goddard lectures at Clark University in the 1920s on his sensational idea that a rocket can fly to the Moon.*

Fortunately, the Smithsonian Institution had been supporting Goddard's work with small grants for several years. In 1919, it published *A Method of Reaching Extreme Altitudes*, Goddard's first report of his discoveries. It could have been called *A Method of Reaching the Moon and Beyond*, since at the very end of the report he gave a brief description of a rocket that could hit the Moon. However, Goddard chose not to concentrate too much on this side of his work, since such speculation could damage his scientific reputation. Instead, his paper focused on the ability of rockets to reach altitudes of about 20 miles (30 km). This was not yet in space, but it was still higher than airplanes and balloons of the day could go. To other scientists, the upper atmosphere was a more respectable goal than space, which was much farther out—in more ways than one. (Space begins at an altitude of roughly 50–100 miles—or 80–160 km—above all but the faintest trace of atmosphere.)

Goddard had decided he would let his dream out a little at a time. Stuntmen like Law could make rocket travel look laughable. Misguided critics could insist on Step B and other presumed problems. And the opinions of fellow scientists could keep Goddard's real rockets temporarily confined to the atmosphere. But the Worcester professor knew that he alone was making serious progress toward the stars.

Or, at least, so he thought, until he received the following letter written in awkward English from a young physicist living in Germany:

Heidelberg, May 3rd, 1922.

Dear Sir,

already many years I work at the problem to pass over the atmosphere of our earth by means of a rocket. When I was now publishing the result of my examination and calculations, I learned by the newspaper, that I am not alone in my inquiries and that you, dear Sir, have already done much important works at this sphere. In spite of my efforts, I did not succeed in getting your books about this object.

Therefore I beg you, dear Sir, to let me have them.—At once after coming out of my work I will be honoured to send it to you, for I think that only by common work of the scholars of all nations can be solved this great problem.

Yours very truly
Hermann Oberth

The Space Race Begins

Robert Goddard was not the only one taking science fiction seriously. In the winter of 1905, when the Worcester college student was seeking the trick that would make space flight possible, Hermann Oberth was an eleven-year-old boy in Transylvania (now part of Romania), reading *From the Earth to the Moon*. Curious to know if the escape velocity used in the story was correct, he calculated it for himself and discovered it was. He also detected the same flaws in Verne's cannon-launch system that Goddard had. And within two years—far sooner than the American—he had run through all the alternatives and settled on rockets as the only practical means of getting into space. "I cannot say that I favored it very much, because of the danger of explosion," he admitted, "but I saw no other way."

Like Goddard, Oberth spent every spare moment thinking about space, and he devoted his education to learning the skills that would help him get there. By 1922, he was on the verge of publishing his results when he heard about Goddard's Smithsonian report. Oberth's letter shows how eager he was to make contact with a fellow enthusiast.

But Goddard was not so eager—especially when he received Oberth's book, *The Rocket into Planetary Space*, the following year. Both men, it turned out, had discovered the same principles and come to the same conclusions, except that Oberth had been much bolder. Goddard only hinted at his real dreams, while Oberth outlined the major details of a human flight beyond Earth.

The two men would soon learn that an even bolder thinker had preceded them both. Working alone in Russia in the late 1800s, a deaf schoolteacher named Konstantin Tsiolkovsky discovered the importance of thrust, exhaust velocities, nozzles, multiple stages, escape velocity, and many other aspects of rockets. He, too, had been inspired by reading *From the Earth to the Moon*. And like Oberth he suggested solutions to the practical problems of human survival on space missions.

As the three rocket scientists gradually learned of each other's work, they discovered that still others had been attacking the problem—in France, Austria, and elsewhere—though none had made as much progress as the American, the Romanian, and the Russian. Even so, more and more solitary thinkers were independently reaching the conclusion that rockets could make the dream of space flight a reality.

"Moonie" Goddard

What did the public make of it? In Russia, few people knew about the deaf schoolteacher. In Germany, where Oberth's book was published, the idea of space travel won an enthusiastic popular audience, though most scientists remained skeptical. And in America, Goddard's Smithsonian report created an unexpected sensation.

"Science to Try Shooting Moon with a Rocket," announced the *Chicago Tribune*. "Modern Jules Verne Invents Rocket to Reach Moon," trumpeted the *Boston American*. Apparently, Goddard's brief example of how a rocket could hit the Moon led many newspapers to assume he was ready to launch any day.

One paper, the *New York Times*, scolded the Worcester scientist for getting his physics wrong: "Professor Goddard . . . does not know the relation of action to reaction, and of the need to have something better than a vacuum against which to

▲ *Konstantin Tsiolkovsky (1857–1935), a village school-teacher in Russia, pioneered the study of rockets as a means of exploring space before either Goddard or Oberth.*

◄ *Working independently in Europe, Hermann Oberth (1894–1989) discovered the principles of rocketry and space travel about the same time as Goddard.*

"So much for the New York Times!"

Students attending the weekly assembly at Clark University in the mid-1920s got an eye-opening physics lesson one day from Professor Robert Goddard.

Appearing with various items of lab equipment, including a .22-caliber revolver, Goddard set up an experiment in which the pistol was attached to a rotating spindle beneath a heavy glass bell jar.

Explaining that he had loaded the gun with a blank cartridge, which would produce a burst of gas, just like a rocket, Goddard proceeded to pump air out of the jar. This created a vacuum, just as in space.

Goddard then posed a question: When the gun is fired in the vacuum by remote control, will it recoil? Next, he read aloud an editorial from the *New York Times* in which the newspaper insisted, in effect: No, because there is no air for the gases to push against. The editorial went on to make fun of Goddard for publicly proposing that rockets would produce a recoil in space and could therefore be used for space travel.

Who was right? Goddard pressed a button, the pistol fired, and it spun around and around the spindle in a splendid demonstration of Newton's third law of action and reaction.

"So much for the *New York Times!*" the professor declared.

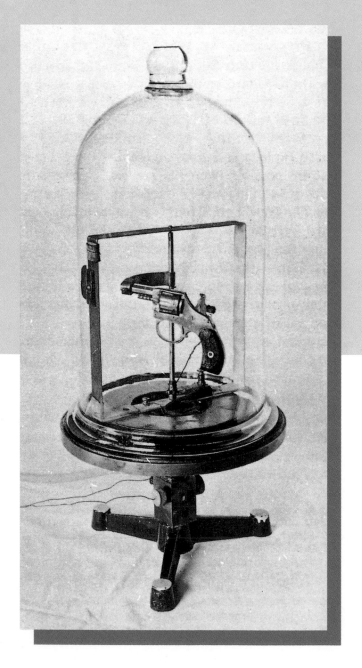

◀ *Professor Goddard's unusual experiment.*

react. . . . Of course he only seems to lack the knowledge ladled out daily in high school." It was Step B again.

The newspaper stories attracted more than a hundred volunteers eager to repeat Rodman Law's exploit, with hopes of better results. A veteran pilot of World War I offered to ride the Goddard rocket to the Moon, or even Mars, if he was given a $10,000 life insurance policy. Goddard also received the following invitation: "As undoubtedly you will desire some special starting point from which to start this rocket . . . the Bronx Exposition, Inc. offers the use of Starlight Amusement Park for the purpose."

"There is, at this moment, no rocket ship contemplated for the Moon," the Worcester professor insisted. "If there were less volunteering and more solid support, I could get along much faster."

All he seemed to get in return was a nickname: "Moonie" Goddard.

A New Type of Rocket

The press and public were only too ready to believe a Moon voyage would soon occur. But Goddard, Oberth, and Tsiolkovsky knew how truly difficult it would be. In their younger days, they, too, had been convinced that space travel would be simple, once the trick was found. Now that the trick had been found, there was much hard work to do—more, even, than the rocket scientists themselves suspected.

As far as hardware, Goddard, Oberth, and Tsiolkovsky stood no closer to space than someone lighting up the sky on the Fourth of July. They had, however, made much progress on paper. One of the biggest problems they solved was finding a way to reduce the weight of a rocket's structure.

Because of the way it burns, a solid material like nitrocellulose or gunpowder must be contained inside a relatively heavy structure. It starts burning at one end, and it keeps burning all the way to the opposite end. As a result, the pressure created by expanding gases must be contained throughout the entire rocket body, which serves as the combustion chamber. This means that the body must be very strong and therefore (at least in Goddard's day, before lightweight structural materials had been developed) very heavy.

Goddard tried to solve this problem by devising a system, similar to a machine gun, that delivered individual cartridges of solid propellant into a small combustion chamber just inside the nozzle. This was the only place that had to withstand the high pressure of combustion and therefore the only heavy piece of structure. However, Goddard could never get the mechanism to work smoothly, and, in any case, it still weighed too much.

Since individual "shots" of propellant wouldn't work, Goddard decided to try a continuous "stream" of propellant—in liquid form. In this type of rocket, the bulk of the vehicle is composed of two thin metal tanks filled with liquid fuel and oxidizer. Pumps or pressurized gas force the two chemicals into a small, sturdy combustion chamber, where they are mixed and ignited. Except for the combustion chamber, the whole contraption is like an eggshell: thin, light, fragile, but as strong as it needs to be.

It sounds simple, but the liquids that produce the highest exhaust velocities must be kept extremely cold. Then when they burn, they produce incredibly high temperatures—hot enough to melt practically any metal. The difficulty of storing and pumping supercold liquids, and then cooling a superhot rocket engine, prevented anyone from attempting to build such a rocket until

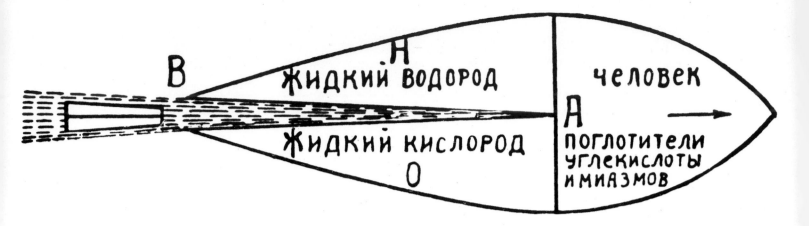

▲ *Published by Tsiolkovsky in 1903, this simplified spaceship design was the first to propose liquid propellants. It features H (liquid hydrogen), O (liquid oxygen), B (a nozzle that ejects the exhaust gases), and A (a crew compartment with environmental controls). Hardly anyone outside of Russia knew of Tsiolkovsky's work.*

Goddard decided there was no other way.

Oberth and Tsiolkovsky had also discovered this revolutionary type of rocket, and they, too, realized there was no other way. Luckily for Goddard, they were much better thinkers than experimenters.

Liquid Air

Like its cousin nitroglycerin, nitrocellulose has a reputation for being explosive beyond belief. In fact, it is less energetic than gasoline. A gasoline-oxygen fire burning in a confined space reaches almost 6,000° Fahrenheit (3,300° C). With a proper nozzle, it produces an exhaust velocity 30 percent faster than nitrocellulose.

However, in order to make an efficient gasoline-oxygen rocket, the oxygen must first be converted into a liquid, which requires cooling it to -298° Fahrenheit (-183° C)—far colder than it ever gets anywhere on Earth. The reason that the oxygen must be converted to liquid is that oxygen (or any other substance) fills much less space in liquid form than it does as a gas. It would be

pointless to build a rocket that carried gaseous oxygen, since the oxidizer tank would have to be enormous. This can be illustrated by looking at how much oxygen is required to burn a full tank of fuel in a car. If the oxygen is reduced to a liquid, it fills a container that can easily fit in the car's backseat; but as a gas, it needs a container as large as an average-size room in a house! Of course, real cars use the oxygen that is readily available in the air around them. Rockets are not so lucky.

In a rocket, liquid oxygen can make pipes crack, gaskets shatter, and valves stick. It can also cause carbon dioxide frost (dry ice) to form, clogging propellant lines. Understandably, Goddard was reluctant to work with such a substance. Yet it was the only way he could see to produce a space rocket. And he knew that once he mastered liquid oxygen and gasoline, he could move on to a far more potent combination: liquid oxygen and liquid hydrogen. These chemicals produce an exhaust velocity 35 percent faster than gasoline and oxygen and almost 80 percent faster than nitrocellulose. The reason Goddard did not immediately try them is that

Propellants

The Chinese who invented rockets a thousand years ago would have no problem recognizing a solid-propellant rocket today. It is still a hollow tube filled with a rapidly burning substance. This is the beauty of solid-propellant rockets: there are no moving parts and therefore only a few things that can go wrong. Unfortunately, if something *does* go wrong, there is no way to stop it. The explosion of the Space Shuttle *Challenger* in 1986 was caused by a leaky joint in a solid-propellant rocket.

On the other hand, liquid-propellant rockets are a plumber's nightmare. But any trouble with them can usually be isolated by turning off valves, which stop the flow of propellant. Liquid propellants also supply more thrust for their weight than most solid propellants, and the rate at which they burn can be controlled much more precisely.

▲ *Assembly of the liquid-propellant tanks for a Titan IV rocket.*

▲ *A Titan IV takes off. The center section uses liquid propellants; the white rockets on either side use solid propellants.*

Right: *Space Shuttle SRB (solid rocket booster). Two such rockets help propel the shuttle during the first two minutes of its journey into space. The propellant, which has the consistency of a pencil eraser, is a combination of ammonium perchlorate (fuel-oxidizer) and small amounts of other ingredients, such as powdered aluminum. **Far right:** Drawn here at the same scale as the SRB, Ariane II is a three-stage, liquid-propellant rocket operated by the European Space Agency. Its first two stages use liquids that can be stored at room temperature and that ignite on contact (no spark is needed). Its third stage uses supercold—and superpowerful—liquid hydrogen and liquid oxygen. Fully fueled, Ariane II and the SRB are both about 90 percent propellant.*

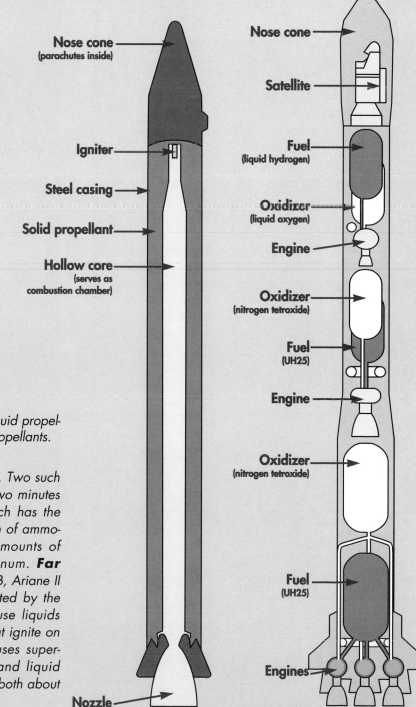

Nose cone
(parachutes inside)

Igniter

Steel casing

Solid propellant

Hollow core
(serves as
combustion chamber)

Nozzle

SRB

Nose cone

Satellite

Fuel
(liquid hydrogen)

Oxidizer
(liquid oxygen)

Engine

Oxidizer
(nitrogen tetroxide)

Fuel
(UH25)

Engine

Oxidizer
(nitrogen tetroxide)

Fuel
(UH25)

Engines

Ariane II

◄ *Atlas-Centaur rockets, one before and one during launch. The rocket's silvery skin has turned a frosty white during take-off due to the supercold liquid oxygen in its tank; also, ice pieces have shaken loose.*

liquid hydrogen is even colder than liquid oxygen, and it presents even greater problems of storage and handling. At the time, it was also nearly impossible to get. However, Goddard could get liquid oxygen (in small amounts from a local industrial supplier), so he started work on what he hoped was the final part of the trick.

Making History

The journey that began in a cherry tree on a splendid autumn day in 1899 reached an important milestone on another day of typical New England weather: a chilly, muddy afternoon at the end of winter, with melting snow all around.

But March 16, 1926, was positively balmy compared to the vapory liquid that Goddard and an assistant carefully poured into a quart-sized (1-liter) container near the base of a very strange-looking contraption. They had brought twice as much liquid oxygen as they needed, knowing that half of the precious oxidizer would boil away as they poured. Beneath the oxidizer tank was a smaller tank, filled with gasoline.

Oddly enough, the rocket's combustion chamber and nozzle were high overhead, supported on a set of pipes leading from the propellant tanks. Goddard had reasoned—incorrectly for a change—that a rocket would be more stable if it was pulled from above rather than pushed from below. (Actually, it makes little difference. His later rockets

would adopt the now-familiar arrangement of combustion chamber and nozzle at the rear.) The vehicle weighed 10.25 pounds (4.65 kg). Of this, about half was fuel and oxidizer. Goddard knew from lab tests that the rocket would produce a steady thrust of nine pounds (4 kg). Since the rocket could not possibly lift off unless the thrust exceeded the weight, some of the propellant would have to burn away and lighten the load before the rocket would budge.

Unfortunately, more than propellant burned away. After ignition, as the vehicle sat roaring in its launch frame for about 20 seconds, the lower part of the nozzle burned through and dropped off. Then the rocket started upward, slowly at first, then faster and faster—like an "express train," thought Goddard—like a "dancer," judged his wife, Esther, who was reminded of a ballerina as the spindly craft gracefully and energetically ascended.

It curved sharply to one side because of the uneven nozzle and landed 184 feet (57 m) away, after rising only 41 feet (13 m) and flying for 2.5 seconds. Goddard wrote up the experiment the following day, recording that history's "first flight with a rocket using liquid propellants was made yesterday at Aunt Effie's farm."

Making News

For the next three years, Aunt Effie's farm was the site of a series of rocket tests, all conducted in secret, until the increasingly noisy experiments could not escape notice. "Terrific Explosion as Prof. Goddard of Clark Shoots His 'Moon

▲ *Goddard just before his successful launch of history's first liquid-propellant rocket on March 16, 1926.*

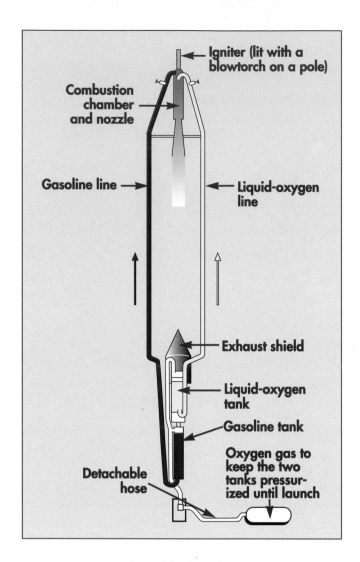

Igniter (lit with a blowtorch on a pole)

Combustion chamber and nozzle

Gasoline line

Liquid-oxygen line

Exhaust shield

Liquid-oxygen tank

Gasoline tank

Oxygen gas to keep the two tanks pressurized until launch

Detachable hose

▲ *Goddard's rocket*

Rocket,'" headlined the *Worcester Evening Post* on July 17, 1929.

Actually, the rocket had only crash-landed after climbing slightly higher than the treetops. There was no explosion. The tremendous roar of the engine, combined with a flame 20 feet (6 m) long shooting from the nozzle, convinced neighbors that a burning airplane had plunged to Earth. The police, ambulances, and reporters all showed up. The state fire marshal was notified. After making an inquiry, he prohibited any further rocket flights in Massachusetts.

The publicity would have been a disaster except that one of the greatest heroes of the day read about the Massachusetts "Moon Man" and guessed he was not the crackpot that the papers implied. Two years earlier, in May 1927, Charles Lindbergh had himself been thought a crackpot—until he succeeded in doing what no one had ever done by piloting an airplane alone across the Atlantic Ocean. Now he was world-famous, with the power to influence the future course of aviation. Lindbergh knew that airplanes would eventually reach the limits of the atmosphere. To go higher, a new type of flying machine was needed.

▲ *This feature story from a 1926 issue of the* Boston Sunday Post *jumped the gun on the Moon race by about forty years. At this point in his career, Goddard had less than ten seconds of flight experience with liquid-propellant rockets. Oberth had no experience.*

Suspecting that the Worcester professor was onto something, Lindbergh set up a meeting. Goddard was astonished to be visited by such a celebrity. Calmly, he explained his work and his goals. "What would help you most?" the famous flier finally asked. Goddard thought for a moment and replied that $25,000 a year for four years would allow him to get established in a suitable location, buy the necessary equipment, hire a few assistants, and accomplish what might otherwise take a lifetime. Convinced that Goddard was on the verge of making a breakthrough as important as the invention of the airplane, Lindbergh arranged for a wealthy family to provide the money. Their support would eventually total $190,000, an enormous sum in those days.

▲ *Goddard (second from left) and his assistants with the remains of a rocket they tested in secret on July 17, 1929. Minutes later, police, ambulances, and reporters arrived.*

Water Rockets

Water rockets are available at toy stores for a few dollars. Buy several and start your own rocket research program.

Try pumping up a rocket with *no* water in it. Then release it. Now fill it *half* full of water and pump it to about the same pressure as before—until you have to push the pump with about the same force (it won't take as many strokes). When you launch the rocket, what's the difference? (Hint: The greater the mass of propellant thrown in one direction, the greater will be the speed of the rocket in the other.)

You can carry out performance tests on water rockets, just as on their more powerful chemical cousins. Here are some ideas:

1. Thrust

To measure the thrust of a water rocket, drill a hole in the top and attach an air-pressure gauge. Bicycle and ball pumps are often equipped with removable pressure gauges. The pressure inside the rocket multiplied by the area at the neck of the nozzle will give its thrust.

Make a list showing the thrust produced by different numbers of pump strokes for different amounts of water. For example: 10, 15, and 20 strokes at ⅛ full; 10, 15, and 20 strokes at ¼ full; ditto at ⅜ full; ditto at ½ full. (Note: This rocket should be used *only* for gathering thrust data; for flight tests, use an identical, unmodified rocket.)

2. Range

Using the above data, test-fly a rocket with different combinations of pump strokes and water amounts. You can gauge the rocket's performance by aiming it at an angle of 45° and measuring its range, or the horizontal distance it travels.

3. Altitude

Stand at a carefully measured distance from the launch site (50 feet—15 m—will do). Holding a protractor modified as shown in the drawing at right, measure the angle of the rocket when it reaches its highest point (the rocket must be shot straight up). Multiply the tangent of the angle times the distance to the launch site: this will give the rocket's altitude. (The tangent can be found on many calculators by entering the angle and punching the "tan" key.)

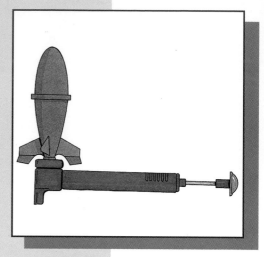

Water rocket

For an airtight seal, drill hole slightly smaller than pressure gauge fitting.

Air-pressure gauge

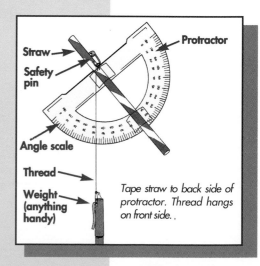

Straw
Safety pin
Protractor
Angle scale
Thread
Weight (anything handy)

Tape straw to back side of protractor. Thread hangs on front side.

Altitude tracker

▲ *Goddard (center) with Charles A. Lindbergh (the tall one at his left), Harry Guggenheim (in the suit), and two assistants—in front of a rocket launch tower in New Mexico in 1935. At Lindbergh's urging, Guggenheim supported Goddard's research throughout most of the 1930s.*

Goddard at last had the freedom to concentrate on achieving his life's dream. In 1930, he and Esther left for the isolated, wide-open spaces of New Mexico—far from the jarring headlines, the nervous neighbors, and the jurisdiction of the state fire marshal of Massachusetts.

The Race Heats Up

Meanwhile, in Germany, rocket fans inspired by reading Oberth's book had banded together in 1927 to raise money for his work. They called their club the Verein für Raumschiffahrt (Society for Spaceship Travel, or VfR), and they also conducted their own research. Oberth's experiments did not get very far, but in 1931, a VfR member succeeded in launching a liquid-propellant rocket. It was thought to be the world's first, since Goddard had kept his own tests with liquids a secret.

Visions of space travel were an exciting distraction from economic and social troubles in Germany that resulted from the nation's defeat in World War I. Many Germans saw rockets as an escape from Earth and its troubles. One such idealist was Wernher von Braun, who joined the VfR as a teenager in 1930, and who closely resembled Goddard in his single-minded ambition to make space flight a reality.

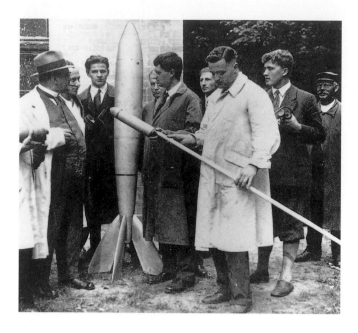

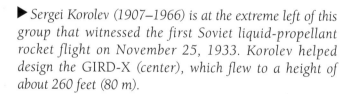

▲ *The VfR president in 1930, Hermann Oberth, stands to the right of a streamlined rocket he developed—but never finished—as a publicity stunt for the 1929 German movie* Woman in the Moon. *The young Wernher von Braun (1912–1977) is to the right of the man holding the pipe rocket.*

▶ *Sergei Korolev (1907–1966) is at the extreme left of this group that witnessed the first Soviet liquid-propellant rocket flight on November 25, 1933. Korolev helped design the GIRD-X (center), which flew to a height of about 260 feet (80 m).*

In the Soviet Union, Tsiolkovsky's writings also led to the formation of space clubs. At one meeting, in 1924, members debated the truth of news reports that Goddard had sent a rocket to the Moon! Space enthusiasts soon got down to the more serious business of perfecting the technology that might someday make such a voyage possible. In 1935, their hero, Tsiolkovsky, died, but he left a legacy of young rocket scientists determined to pursue his ideas. One was a brilliant engineer named Sergei Korolev, who would eventually prove that he combined the vision, inventive genius, and leadership of the best of the rocket pioneers. More and more contestants were getting involved in a race that Goddard had thought he was running alone. But as political turmoil spread across Europe, and nations began arming in fearful anticipation of another world war, dreams of space flight took a backseat to more earthly concerns, and the contestants, one by one, dropped from sight.

After 1938, Goddard heard little more about his rocket competitors abroad.

▶ *A scene from the science fiction film* Woman in the Moon. *Though inspired by Oberth's writings, the movie was full of mistakes—such as omitting space suits on the Moon. It had an impact on real life, however, by inventing the rocket countdown.*

▲ *One of Goddard's rockets being readied for launch in New Mexico, 1940.*

▲ *Launch, 1938.*

To Earth Orbit . . . and Beyond

In September 1944, World War II entered its sixth year of brutal conflict, involving Germany, Japan, and their allies on one side, and Great Britain, the Soviet Union, the United States, and their allies on the other. Billions of bullets, artillery shells, and bombs had filled the battlefields with bodies and the cities with rubble. There seemed to be nothing else that technology could do to increase the ruin of war.

But on September 8, two mysterious explosions shook London. No enemy aircraft were overhead, and the only warning was a high-pitched whistling sound. The explosions continued almost daily. On November 8, the Germans announced they had been bombarding London with a new type of weapon, which they called the V-2 (for Vengeance Weapon 2). The V-1, used earlier in the year, had been an explosives-laden robot plane. The V-2 appeared to be a rocket more powerful than any ever known.

The Toy Grows Up

When the V-2s began to fall, Goddard was almost sixty-two years old. He was working for the U.S. Navy, designing rocket boosters to help seaplanes take off with heavy loads. The military could come up with nothing else for the world's most experienced and creative rocket scientist to do, since they had no interest in long-range rockets.

That is, until the Germans began shooting off the V-2. That weapon came too late to help its inventors, but even before Germany surrendered in May 1945, the United States and the Soviet Union were pondering the importance of rockets to future wars. The toy had grown up.

How much it had grown became apparent to Goddard in March 1945, when he inspected a captured V-2 that had been shipped to America. He compared every detail with his own lifetime of stubborn struggle. His P (for pump) series of rockets—the last built in New Mexico before he joined the war effort in 1942—featured miniature high-pressure pumps to force liquid propellants into the combustion chamber for rapid burning. These rockets included other innovations that Goddard had developed over the

◀ *A V-2 takes off for its target.*

years—such as a method of cooling the combustion chamber to keep it from melting, a gyroscope to keep the rocket on course, movable air vanes and blast vanes to steer the rocket, fins for stabilization, and a streamlined outer skin.

The V-2 had all of these features, plus it was larger—much larger. But the big difference was that it worked.

Goddard tested all his rocket components to make sure they would work, too. But during a flight, when all the parts had to work together, they seldom did. Something almost always went wrong. Goddard didn't consider it a failure when a valve broke, a pump quit, an engine exploded, or any of dozens of other mishaps occurred. He usually learned something from it. He knew he could reach space only by perfecting the complicated hardware that would enable a rocket to produce high thrust with low weight. But it was proving more difficult than he ever imagined.

In 1903, two brothers from Ohio invented the airplane in a similar way: by attacking each part of the problem, making mistakes, and learn-

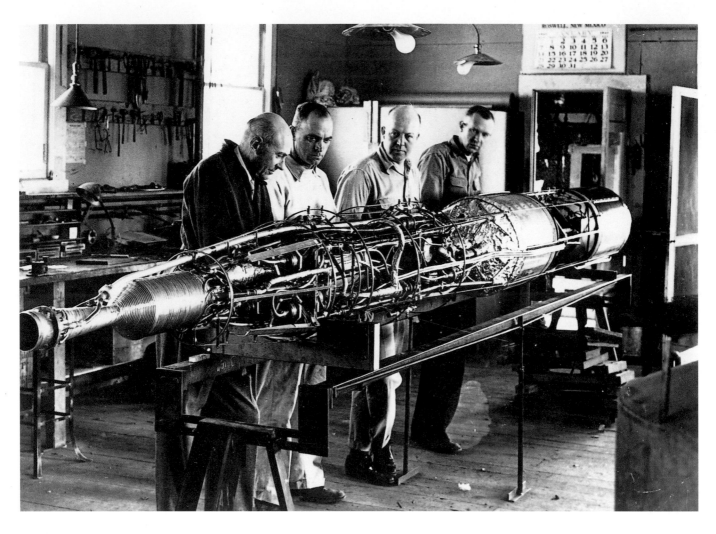

▲ *In 1940, Goddard and his men were working on what they believed to be the largest, most complex rockets ever built.*

ing from them. The Wright brothers did it in their own shop, mostly by themselves. Though a space rocket was turning out to be a much harder problem than an airplane, Goddard had more people working on it (usually about five, including himself), and he had more research money than the Wrights did. But these resources were not nearly enough.

Secret Weapon

By 1933, the members of the VfR in Germany had concluded that their rocket experiments had gone about as far as they could go. In the course of about a hundred flights with liquid propellants, the VfR had achieved a top altitude of 3,000 feet (900 m). Further work, one member noted, "would have been too expensive for any organization, except a millionaires' club." But then a millionaires' club—or what amounted to one—stepped in. It was the German Army. After its defeat in World War I, Germany was restricted by treaty from building a large military force. However, the treaty did not cover rockets. So in the late 1920s, the German Army began investi-

▲ *Meanwhile, Germany was creating a rocket that was far bigger: the V-2.*

gating this new type of technology, paying careful attention to what the VfR and other rocket clubs were doing. The Army concluded that rockets using liquid propellants might make excellent long-range weapons.

In 1932, the Army secretly hired Wernher von Braun to be the technical director of its program. Von Braun soon recruited other VfR members. (Oberth was back in Romania teaching school by this time and would eventually play only a minor role in the effort that his writings had inspired.) Over the course of the next decade, enormous resources, amounting to billions of dollars, were poured into rocket research. Hundreds and ultimately thousands of people were employed designing, building, and testing rockets—all in secret.

The result, as Londoners learned on September 8, 1944, was the V-2. Taking off from German-occupied Holland, the missile reached a top speed of 3,600 miles per hour (5,800 km/h) in just over a minute. Then it arched over the English Channel to a high point of about 60 miles (100 km) before plummeting to the ground. Its explosive warhead could demolish a building. Several thousand were launched before the end of the war, killing many thousands of people.

End of a Dream

"Here is a *space* rocket!" Goddard must have thought as he examined the V-2. Indeed, during one test in Germany, a V-2 had reportedly ascended straight up instead of at the usual angle. On that flight, it traveled well into space, climbing to 120 miles (190 km) before falling to Earth. Goddard's highest flight had reached only 1.4 miles (2.3 km)—about one-hundredth the distance.

Even so, Goddard couldn't help suspecting that the Germans had copied his ideas. "It looks like ours," one of his New Mexico assistants observed. But the Germans had simply faced the same problems and come up with the same solutions. They had wracked their brains, too. And just as Goddard, Oberth, and Tsiolkovsky had each discovered that rockets alone offered the best hope of reaching space, the technology of the day did not offer many solutions for designing rockets that could actually get there. One inescapable conclusion was that it was a task beyond the capabilities of a small team. Goddard and his crew might just as well have tried to build the Golden Gate Bridge or Boulder Dam—two gigantic engineering projects of the day. The methods of Edison and the Wright brothers were no longer enough. For all his brilliance, Goddard was a nineteenth-century scientist trying to tackle a twentieth-century problem.

Goddard did not live much beyond his glimpse of the first space rocket. By the summer, his health was failing from cancer. "I don't think he ever got over the V-2," a friend recalled. The dreamer who gazed into the sky every October 19, and thought about *The War of the Worlds* and a bright idea that came all of a sudden from the branches of a cherry tree, died on August 10, 1945.

Bigger, Faster, Farther

Goddard died just as the most terrible weapon ever devised became known. On August 6 and 9, 1945, atomic bombs were dropped on Japan, bringing a decisive end to World War II. As a weapon, the nuclear bomb was far more successful than the V-2, and it would lead to the development of even bigger rockets—ones that could finally achieve Goddard's dream.

From the military's point of view, the problem with the V-2 was that it was not accurate enough; it could destroy a building, but not a specific building. However, when armed with a nuclear bomb, a rocket could destroy an entire city, so accuracy hardly mattered. What did matter was range. The V-2 had a range of 200 miles (320 km). After World War II, military strategists in the United States and the Soviet Union began to draw up plans for rockets that could loft nuclear bombs for thousands of miles, across entire continents—at each other.

Such intercontinental missiles would need to be much larger than the V-2, and they would need several stages in order to reach speeds that

Model Rockets

This sequence of eight movie frames shows ⅓ second in the early moments of a model rocket launch. Knowing that the rocket is 36 inches (91 cm) tall, you can calculate that it is moving 11 miles per hour (18 km/h) between the first and second frames (at the top of the page), and 31 miles per hour (50 km/h) between the last two frames (at the bottom of the page).

The rate of increase in velocity is called acceleration. By the time the solid rocket motor runs out of propellant, about ½ second after the bottom frame, the rocket will be traveling faster than an Indianapolis racecar, at which point it will be only 200 feet (60 m) or so in the air. However, its energy will keep propelling it upward until gravity and air resistance slow it to zero, at an altitude of more than 2,000 feet (600 m), and it begins to fall to Earth—with a parachute.

Model rockets are an excellent tool for investigating the principles of rocketry. You can get the materials for a model rocket at many hobby stores or by contacting the National Association of Rocketry (NAR) for a list of suppliers: NAR, Box 177, Altoona, WI 54720.

(0.13 sec. after liftoff)

(0.42 sec. after liftoff)

▲ The author deploys recovery forces for a three-stage model rocket launch. Ignition was with an electrical igniter connected to a car battery.

▲ Reading from top to bottom, a model rocket streaks aloft powered by a few ounces of solid propellant. The frames are ¼₄ second apart. Interestingly, the rocket decelerates (its velocity drops) between frames 2, 3, and 4, before accelerating again—probably because it was snagged briefly on the tip of the launch rod. The height of the rocket is 36 inches (91 cm).

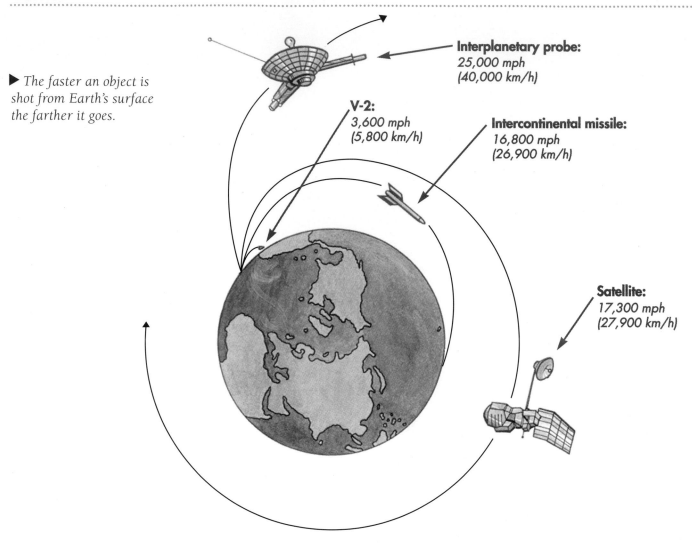

▶ *The faster an object is shot from Earth's surface the farther it goes.*

Interplanetary probe:
25,000 mph
(40,000 km/h)

V-2:
3,600 mph
(5,800 km/h)

Intercontinental missile:
16,800 mph
(26,900 km/h)

Satellite:
17,300 mph
(27,900 km/h)

would allow them to coast around much of the planet. Whether the strategists realized it or not, such missiles would also solve another problem with the V-2: that although it could get into space, it didn't have enough speed to stay there.

In order to travel a third of the way around Earth—8,300 miles (13,300 km)—an intercontinental missile must ascend to an altitude of about 190 miles (300 km), turn to an angle of 15 degrees above the horizon, and reach a speed of 16,800 miles per hour (26,900 km/h) before exhausting its propellant. By traveling just a bit faster—17,300 miles per hour (27,900 km/h)—and aiming exactly horizontal, the mis-

sile will do something very interesting: it will coast completely around Earth, not once, but over and over, in a path called an orbit. Such an orbiting vehicle is called a "satellite."

Depending on the altitude, a satellite can orbit Earth more or less indefinitely, but it is still bound by Earth's gravity. However, by traveling at a speed of at least 25,000 miles per hour (40,000 km/h), an object can escape Earth altogether and set off for the Moon or planets. This is escape velocity— the goal that had preoccupied Goddard, Oberth, and Tsiolkovsky.

Military planners in the United States and the Soviet Union were not interested in having anything escape Earth or even go into orbit, despite the fact that they were developing missiles that could achieve these feats. But two of their key rocket scientists *were* interested: von Braun, who had emigrated to America after World War II with his German rocket team; and Korolev, the Russian engineer who had been inspired by Tsiolkovsky. Both found themselves pursuing space travel through the back door of military projects for their governments.

Testing the Water

In 1949, an important milestone was reached when the United States launched a captured V-2 with a second stage instead of the usual warhead. The small upper-stage rocket, which was ignited

Goddard P Series

Goddard's last series of rockets tested a new type of pump to force propellants into the combustion chamber. It performed the job much more efficiently than pressurized gas, which he used in earlier rockets. Such pumps allow liquid-propellant rockets to achieve very high thrust with low weight. Goddard did not live to perfect this important development.

Stages: *1*
Propellant: *gasoline/liquid oxygen*
Total weight: *440 pounds (200 kg)*
Percentage propellant: *55%*
First flight: *1940*
Highest flight: *300 feet (90 m)*

Goddard rocket

after the V-2's propellant ran out, reached a speed of 5,150 miles per hour (8,290 km/h) and an altitude of 244 miles (390 km). For the first time, one rocket had boosted another above the limits of the atmosphere. Though far short of orbital velocity, the flight demonstrated that rockets could travel ever faster and deeper into space. Even so, most people continued to think of space travel—whether by machines or humans—as science fiction.

Frustrated by this attitude, von Braun began writing popular articles about Earth-orbiting space stations and trips to the Moon and Mars, showing how society was on the verge of achieving an incredible dream. By the mid-1950s, he came close to convincing the U.S. government to let him use an Army missile to launch a satellite. But the government decided there was no rush.

Korolev's Giant

In the Soviet Union, work on long-range rockets was proceeding even more quickly than in the United States. Unlike the Americans, the Soviets did not have a large bomber fleet, and rockets offered the only sure means of delivering nuclear weapons in the event of another world war.

Leading the Soviet effort, Korolev developed a monstrous intercontinental missile—the R-7—which operated in two stages with a total of twenty main combustion chambers, each nearly equal in thrust to the single combustion chamber of a V-2. Korolev's giant was as tall as three buses stacked end to end, and it

▲ *A V-2 with a second stage added.*

weighed more than twenty fully loaded buses. Ninety percent of it was liquid propellant (compared to 70 percent for the V-2 and 55 percent for Goddard's P series). When the R-7 was ignited, the ground shook and night turned to day.

Arguing that his rocket did little good as a military threat unless other countries knew it existed, Korolev convinced Soviet leaders that a satellite launch would serve as impressive proof. On October 4, 1957, the giant missile hurled a simple spacecraft called Sputnik into orbit and impressed the world in ways that no one had predicted.

V-2

A captured German V-2 is readied for a test at White Sands, New Mexico, in the late 1940s.

Stages: *1*
Propellant: *alcohol/liquid oxygen*
Total weight: *28,400 pounds (12,900 kg)*
Percentage propellant: *70%*
First flight: *1942*
Highest flight: *130 miles (210 km)—in a U.S. test in 1951*

Goddard rocket   **V-2**

▲ *Twenty big engines, plus twelve smaller ones, had to ignite all at once whenever Korolev's giant thundered to life. Two minutes into the flight, the four outer pods (the first stage) dropped away. The rocket shown here is a three-stage version, like the one used to launch the first human in space in 1961.*

Aiming at the Stars

Though Goddard, Oberth, Tsiolkovsky, von Braun, Korolev, and others had been working toward this goal for decades, the start of the space age took most people by surprise. Few suspected that the Soviets were capable of such a feat. Besides, the world was waiting for a trick that would make space travel as easy as travel across the ground or through the air.

Sputnik proved that space travel is different. It's harder. And getting into space is the hardest part of all. It took a vehicle weighing almost 600,000 pounds (270,000 kg) to get the 184-pound (84-kg) Sputnik into orbit. What would it take to get a human into orbit? Or to the Moon? Or Mars? It wouldn't be easy, but Sputnik had shown the way. With it came the

◀ *America reacts to Sputnik.*

realization that a simple principle, demonstrated by an age-old toy, and applied on an enormous scale, could do the job. Sputnik was the starting gun in a hotly contested space race between the Soviet Union and the United States. Military rockets were turned toward winning public-opinion victories in space. Given a quick go-ahead, von

R-7 (Sputnik Launcher)

Known to Russian rocket engineers as *Semyorka* (which translates as "Old Number Seven"), this vehicle was the world's first successful satellite launcher. An improved version with three stages is still used by Russia.

Stages: 2 *(four pods, with engines and propellant tanks, drop away in flight)*
Propellant: *kerosene/ liquid oxygen*
Total weight: *589,000 pounds (268,000 kg)*
Percentage propellant: *90%*
First flight: *1957*
Highest flight: *1,200 miles (1,900 km)*

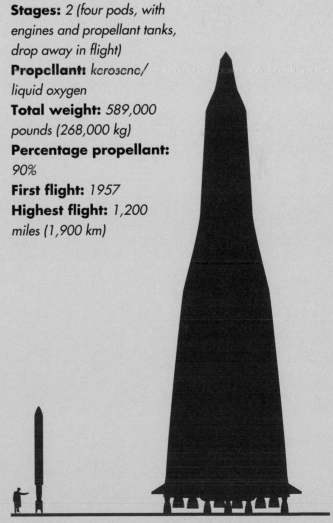

Goddard rocket

R-7

Braun was able to launch an American satellite by January 1958. More Soviet and American satellites soon followed. Korolev added a third stage to his giant and made it capable of accomplishing a feat for which newspapers had ridiculed Goddard forty years earlier: On September 14, 1959, he hit the Moon with a small spacecraft intended to show that Russians could get there first.

Almost without thinking, the United States and the Soviet Union adopted a goal that only novelists and dreamers had dared discuss before: a human flight to the Moon. Throughout the 1960s, Americans and Soviets raced to be first to a series of checkpoints that marked the

Saturn V

The huge rocket that launched people to the Moon was originally considered too small to do the job alone. *Two* of these monsters were judged necessary to get the required spaceship parts into Earth orbit, where they would be connected and launched to the Moon. At least, that was the thinking in 1961, when U.S. President John F. Kennedy officially set the goal of "landing a man on the Moon and returning him safely to Earth." At the time, the Saturn V didn't exist yet.

"Returning safely to Earth" was the hard part. The crew-occupied portion of the spaceship had to carry not only enough propellant to land on the Moon but also enough to get back home. Since a booster to launch such a vehicle would be impractically large, the best strategy seemed to be to use two Saturn V's to launch the ship in pieces for assembly in space. Such maneuvers had never been tried.

Then engineers came up with a clever idea. Why take the entire crew cabin to the Moon's surface? After all, when Columbus arrived in America he didn't beach his flagship—he anchored it in deep water and took a rowboat

▲ *The LM (in the background) with the cargo it brought to the Moon on the Apollo 15 mission in 1971.*

ashore. The rowboat became the "LM"—the lunar module. The flagship, which would remain in lunar orbit while the LM went down to the surface, was the "CM"—the command module. The beauty of the plan was that the LM didn't need to journey all the way back to Earth; it could be left behind in lunar orbit after the Moon walkers rocketed back to the CM. The weight savings meant that a single Saturn V could do the job.

Like so much else in the history of space flight, when others set out to solve the same problem,

Stages: *3*
Propellant: *kerosene/liquid oxygen (stage 1); liquid hydrogen/liquid oxygen (stages 2 and 3)*
Total weight: *6,400,000 pounds (2,900,000 kg)*
Percentage propellant: *88%*
First flight: *1967*
Highest flight: *the Moon*

they came up with the same solution—for the Soviets, too, adopted this strategy for their lunar landing program.

However, in the end, only the United States succeeded in perfecting a Moon rocket. Between 1969 and 1972, von Braun's Saturn V sent six teams of astronauts to the Moon's surface on what were surely history's most incredible voyages of discovery.

Goddard rocket

Saturn V

▲ *Goddard (right) and his men retrieve a rocket after a disappointing test on April 19, 1932. The next day, Goddard wrote to thank author H. G. Wells for inspiring a boy in Massachusetts, many years earlier, to pursue a career "aiming at the stars."*

"I think it's fair to say you haven't seen anything yet," Goddard predicted in 1945. Reusable shuttles, photos beamed from the farthest planets, space telescopes, space stations, and other amazing achievements since the Moon landings have shown that Goddard's words are as true today as ever. Who knows what wonders the future holds?

In the midst of his experiments in the New Mexico desert in the 1930s, Goddard sat down to thank the man who had inspired his life's work. "In 1898 I read your *War of the Worlds*," he wrote to H. G. Wells. The rocket pioneer went on to describe the twists and turns his career had taken, and how a spellbinding story about an invasion from Mars had never left him, and never would. He continued:

How many more years I shall be able to work on the problem, I do not know; I hope as long as I live. There can be no thought of finishing, for 'aiming at the stars' . . . is a problem to occupy generations, so that no matter how much progress one makes, there is always the thrill of just beginning.

Resources

Books on Rockets and Space

The Cambridge Encyclopedia of Space (New York, 1990). This one-volume reference book does a thorough job covering the history of space exploration. Rocket technology, orbits, and space hardware are dealt with in great detail. Heavily illustrated.

Frederick I. Ordway III and Randy Liebermann, editors, *Blueprint for Space: Science Fiction to Science Fact* (Washington, 1992). Chapters by different authors describe the progression of space flight from dream to reality.

G. Harry Stine, *Handbook of Model Rocketry* (New York, 1987). An excellent guide to the theory and practice of model rocketry.

George P. Sutton, *Rocket Propulsion Elements* (New York, 1992). For advanced rocketeers interested in the details of how actual rocket engines are designed.

Frank H. Winter, *Rockets into Space* (Cambridge, 1990). A concise history of rockets with a discussion of the contributions of Goddard, Oberth, Tsiolkovsky, and other pioneers.

Books on Goddard

Karin Clafford Farley, *Robert H. Goddard* (Englewood Cliffs, 1991). A biography of Goddard, aimed at grades 5–9.

Esther C. Goddard, editor, *The Papers of Robert H. Goddard* (New York, 1970). Available through libraries, this three-volume illustrated work traces Goddard's research in his own words—in diary entries, lab notes, reports, and letters. Very interesting to browse through.

Milton Lehman, *Robert H. Goddard: Pioneer of Space Research* (New York, 1988). The most complete biography of Goddard yet written.

Museums

National Air and Space Museum, Washington, D.C. (Tel.: (202) 357-1686). The world's most popular museum, featuring many of the rockets mentioned in this book, plus exhibits on the principles of rocketry.

Roswell Museum and Art Center, Roswell, New Mexico (Tel.: (505) 624-6744). Here, Goddard's workshop has been re-created in the town where he conducted his most ambitious experiments. Outside is the launch tower shown on page 53.

U.S. Space and Rocket Center, Huntsville, Alabama (Tel.: (205) 837-3400). Best known for hosting the U.S. Space Camp, this museum also has an extensive collection of rockets and spacecraft, including an actual Saturn V and a full-size mock-up of the Space Shuttle.

Electronic Media

Rocket Designer (Tony Wayne, Albemarle High School, Charlottesville, Virginia 22901). An easy-to-use computer program for designing model rockets. Requires a Macintosh with a 12-inch color monitor, 1.5 megs of RAM, and HyperCard 2.1.

The Rocket Men: Robert Goddard and the Adventure of Space Exploration (Goldhil Home Media, Thousand Oaks, California 91360). First broadcast on the Disney Channel in 1994, this hour-long video is an engaging portrait of Goddard. Includes home movies of his rocket tests and reminiscences by his wife, Esther.